THE ART *of* STRIPES

CONTENTS

The timeless marinière shirt – worn by beaucoup handsome French sailors, Coco Chanel, Audrey Hepburn and James Dean – has earned its place in the fashion hall of fame.

As contemporary designers draw inspiration from the nautical design, this book shows how to add stripes to your look; revealing the ultimate Breton brands, and ten inspirational stripe-wearing icons from silvery-haired stylist Linda Rodin to a punky 1980s Madonna from the wrong side of the tracks.

A modern essential to your wardrobe, discover the surprising history – and how to look great in – the world's chicest design.

MASTER THE ART OF STRIPES!

STRIPES IN STYLE

How the Breton Top Earned its Stripes.

Devotees of fashion astrology take note: on March 27th 1858, something rather auspicious happened in the world of stripes. In Bretagne, northern France, a decree was signed, introducing a three-quarter length sleeved striped shirt as the official seaman's uniform. Crafted for practicality (and, seemingly, a little French cool), the long length covered a sailor's lower back and a boat neck offered ease of movement.

The rules were simple yet exact: 21 white stripes (20 mm/¾ in wide), front and back, each twice as wide as the 20 navy stripes (10 mm/⅓ in), plus 14 navy stripes on the arms. This 1800s version of hi-vis was soon made the uniform of the French navy. Known as the marinière or tricot rayé, the shirts were eventually made in army clothing workshops (often by conscripts) and became synonymous with French culture.

Then, in the 1920s, Coco Chanel added the classic marinière to her boutiques, giving the traditional workwear garment a little je ne c'est quoi, and by the 30s, 40s, and 50s the Breton stripe became a way to signify an artistic, inventive, and bohemian spirit. Stripe-wearers like James Dean, Truman Capote, Audrey Hepburn and Jean Seberg helped give the Breton its counter cultural, bad boy status, and it later found fans in Johnny Ramone, Bob Dylan, Kurt Cobain – oh, and Kate Middleton.

Much like its workwear cousins: denim jeans, the worker jacket, and the military parka, the stripe top is a wardrobe essential. A shortcut to thoughtful chic with a little underground edge, the Breton has earned its stripes.

Some heart-stopping stripe moments: Jean Seberg in *Breathless*, James Dean in *Rebel Without a Cause*, Edie Sedgwick at Warhol's Factory, Cary Grant in *To Catch a Thief* (with a red bandana underneath), and Hugh Hefner in his playboy dressing gown.

3 SIMPLE WAYS TO STYLE A

Breton Top

Black and white stripes are often thought of as the neutral of the pattern world because they pair beautifully with just about everything. A simple striped boatneck can be the anchor for so many styles. Whether paired with a trench coat and denim for a Saturday in Soho or red silk and stilettos for a night at the symphony, stripes make the perfect accent.

1
Work Day

Start with a striped boatneck, then add a chambray shirt, pastel wool miniskirt, black tights, leather booties, and a soft black leather satchel.

2
Weekend Play

Start with a striped boatneck, then add a khaki trench, relaxed cuffed denim, black canvas sneakers, and an oversized ivory leather shoulder bag.

3
Date Night

Start with a striped boatneck, then add a monochrome midi skirt and matching silk scarf around a chignon or loose ponytail, a sleek black wristlet, and black ankle-strap heels.

START WITH A

Bell Sleeve Top

THEN ADD:

vertical-striped culottes

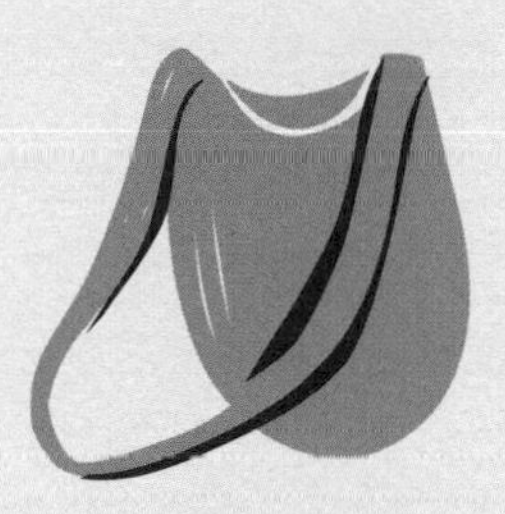

soft, leather hobo bag

colourful strappy heels

START WITH A

Colourfully Striped Popover

THEN ADD:

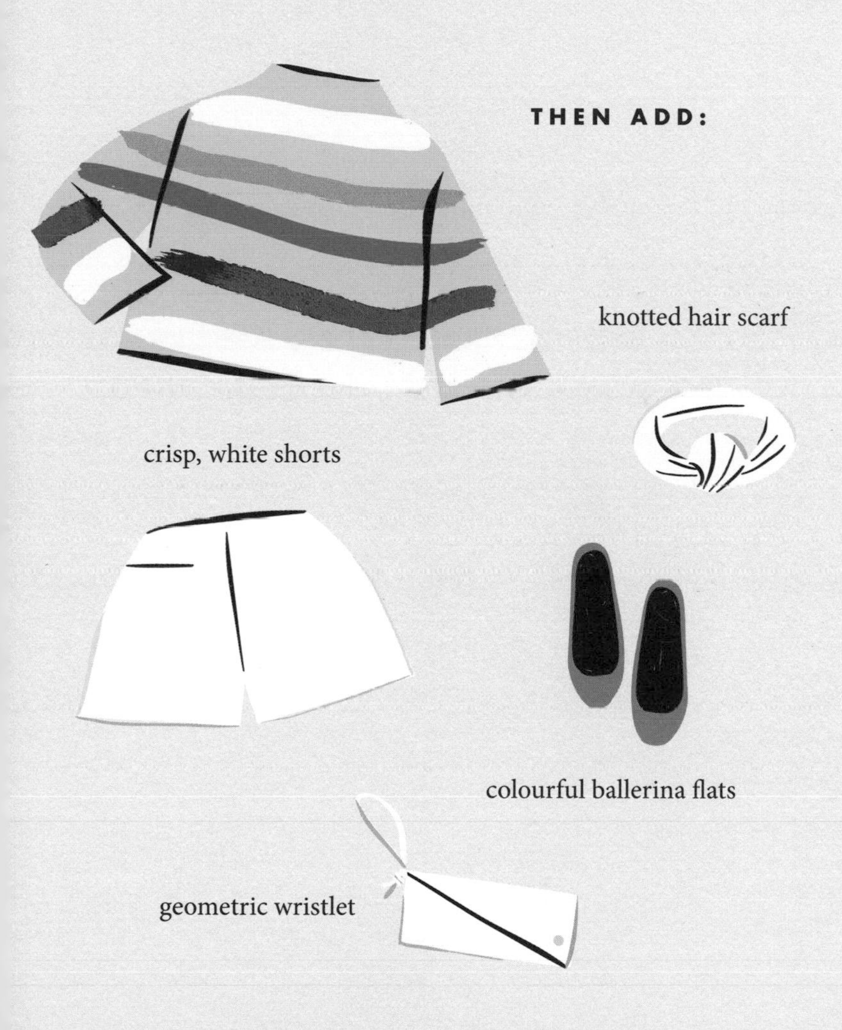

START WITH A

Fitted Striped Mock Turtleneck

THEN ADD:

Style Icon

CAROLINE DE MAIGRET

The slouchy, sexy and purely Parisian style of music producer and model Caroline de Maigret has become one of the most frothed over in the age of street style (652K Instagram followers, anyone?); she is a touchstone for contemporary brands who are obsessed by her effortless approach to looking good.

When she's not walking for mega brands like Chanel, she's popping out for a baguette on her scooter in her ultimate hang out outfit: loose, striped men's shirt, ripped and faded slim-not-skinny vintage jeans, white sneaks, and a beautifully battered leather biker – oh, and the world's finest set of bangs. She loves Keith Richards (you can see little references to him in her style), and always adds a louche, off-duty rockstar edge to her every day outfits. Naturally, stripes feature in de Maigret's most memorable looks from oversized men's shirts, to thick colour block pieces, to traditional Breton tops – and she looks amazing in them all.

As one of the authors of *How to be a Parisian Wherever You Are*, she's full of easy tips and chic life hacks, from recommending designers like Haider Ackermann, investing in the perfect high waist jeans by Sonia Rykiel, to vintage Saint Laurent finds, and sleeping in a braid to give your hair that just-been-shagged look. More importantly, de Maigret is empowered by the idea of accepting your imperfections and not letting yourself down; where even banal trips to walk the dog or buy toilet paper can be done in a mindful and subtly chic way.

START WITH AN

Oversized Striped Cotton Sweater

THEN ADD:

cut off denim shorts

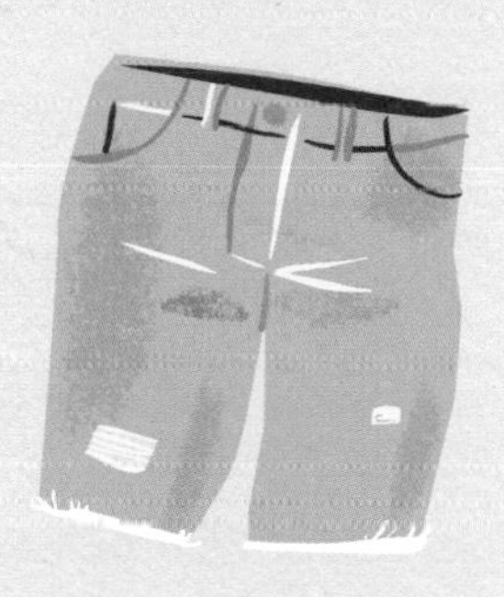

tortoise sunglasses

leather-strapped straw totc

white canvas tennis shoes

START WITH A

Bold Pinstripe Blouse

THEN ADD:

START WITH AN

Oversized Striped Pocket T

THEN ADD:

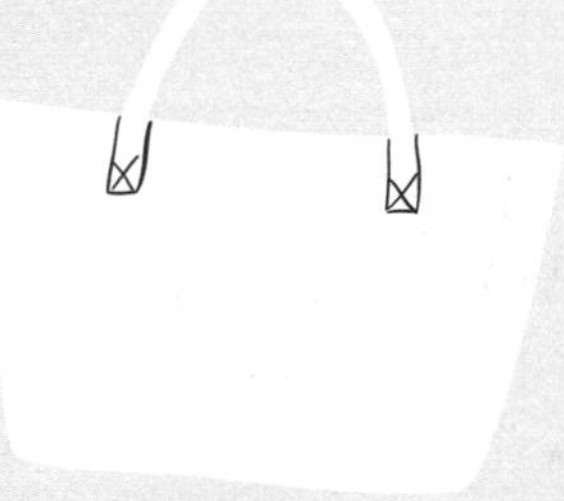

canvas utility tote

camel hair cocoon coat

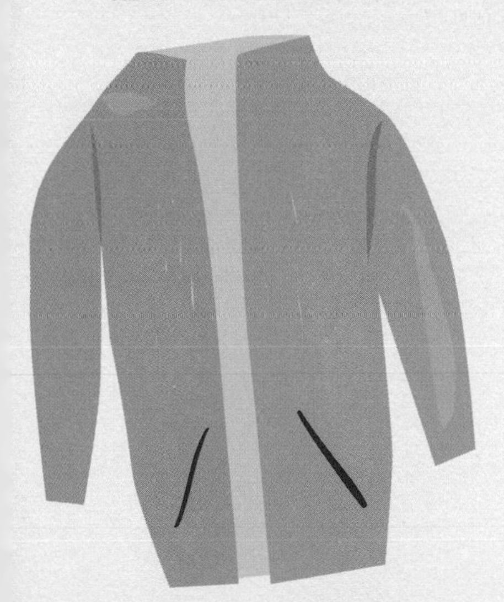

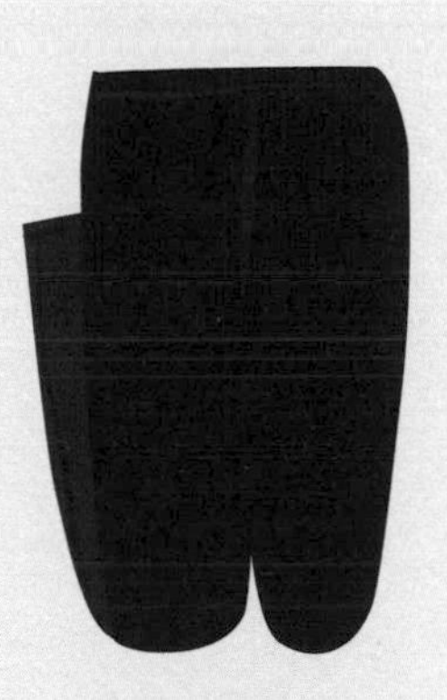

black leggings

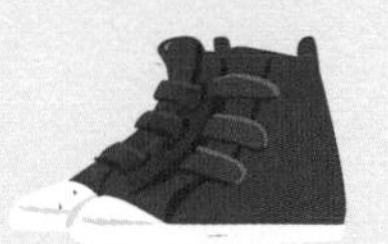

leather hi-tops

Style Icon

BIANCA JAGGER

Floppy trilbys, feathered and bejewelled turbans, boob-baring tuxedo jackets, and a dazzle of stripes: Bianca Jagger can even accessorise a naked gold-glitter giant and real-life horse into her disco-dancing ensemble (as the Studio 54 legend goes). Some can wear anything – literally anything – and still look nothing less than amazing. The model and activist is one of those people.

Born in Nicaragua in 1945, Jagger studied political science in Paris, and kept a healthy balance between human rights work and hanging out at the best parties in the world. A wonderfully androgynous, glamorous and louche dresser, by the late 60s Jagger became known for her style; she was synonymous with Yves Saint Laurent's Le Smoking (the world's most elegant, most practical women's suit), and her marriage to Mick Jagger in 1971 helped secure her icon status.

Stripes and suits have continued to be a major presence in Jagger's personal style arsenal, from sequined strapless dresses to Breton tops; she continues to be a tastemaker. She loves platform shoes, Cartier earrings, cashmere scarves – and encouraging the use of social media to help affect political change from the ground, up. In this way, Jagger has an exciting duality. As an icon, not only does she have impeccable, unpretentious style, her award-winning human rights work is truly inspiring.

START WITH A

Skinny Striped T-Shirt

THEN ADD:

oversized pleated silk trousers

white leather shoulder bag with contrasting strap

black heeled loafers

START WITH

Sleek Striped Trousers

THEN ADD:

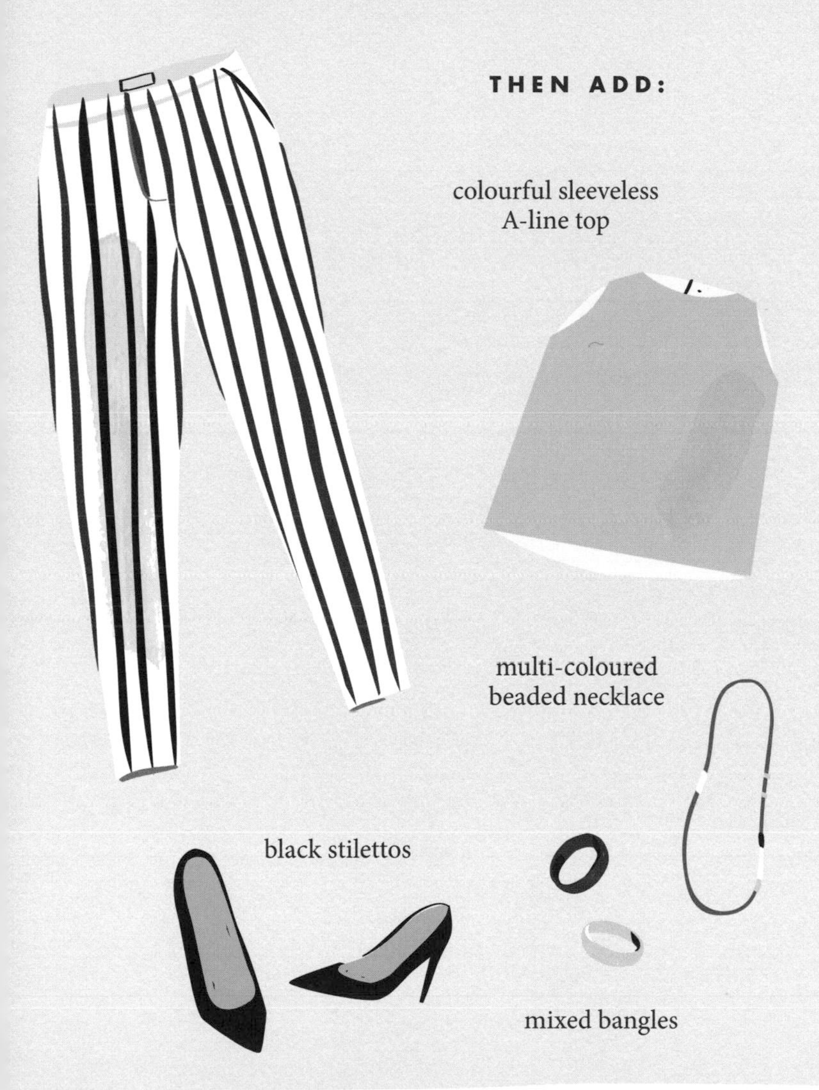

colourful sleeveless A-line top

multi-coloured beaded necklace

black stilettos

mixed bangles

START WITH A

Striped Cotton Boatneck

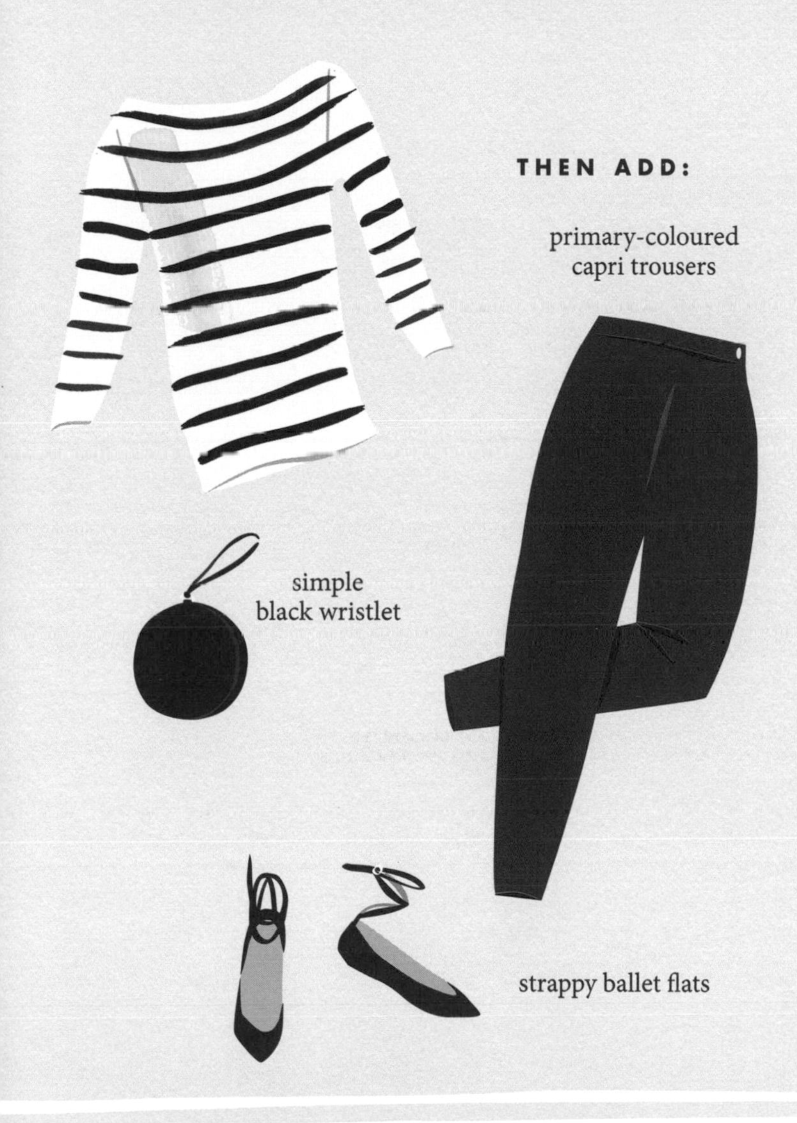

Style Icon

BRIGITTE BARDOT

The Frenchiest French woman who ever lived, Brigitte Bardot is an alumni of the Serge Gainsbourg school of sexual controversy. As muse to the saucy 60s pop chanteur, Bardot became Gainsbourg's partner in crime; the pair appeared on a number of albums together, a collaboration that arguably helped her secure her pop culture and sex symbol status.

A trained ballerina, Bardot appeared in a number of comedy romps in her youth, but it was ... *And God Created Woman* in 1956 that shot Bardot to international stardom; in it she played the late 1950s version of a hot mess, a gorgeous beach bum sexpot. Images of Bardot on every beach in France resurfaced, and helped secure her fame – and popularise the bikini. The double-cold shoulder neckline is known in the fashion biz as the Bardot, named after her penchant for sexy, almost-falling-off outfits. But it's the Breton stripe – the nautical-inspired design – that's just as an essential element to Bardot's most enduring outfits. In fact, contemporary style has much to thank Bardot for. The loose beehive? Bardot. The open neck top and cropped pant combo? Brigitte. The dark cat-eye makeup and floppy beach hat? You guessed it.

Like most enduring icons, Brigitte Bardot found a look that worked for her – and stuck to it. Luckily, there's an easy way to nail Bardot's naughty-and-nautical, St Tropez look. Slip on a Breton top, accessorise with a quiet confidence, wind-ruffled hair, and affect the air of a languorous, leggy French sex symbol.

START WITH A

Striped Raglan Sweatshirt

THEN ADD:

START WITH

High Contrast Striped Stockings

THEN ADD:

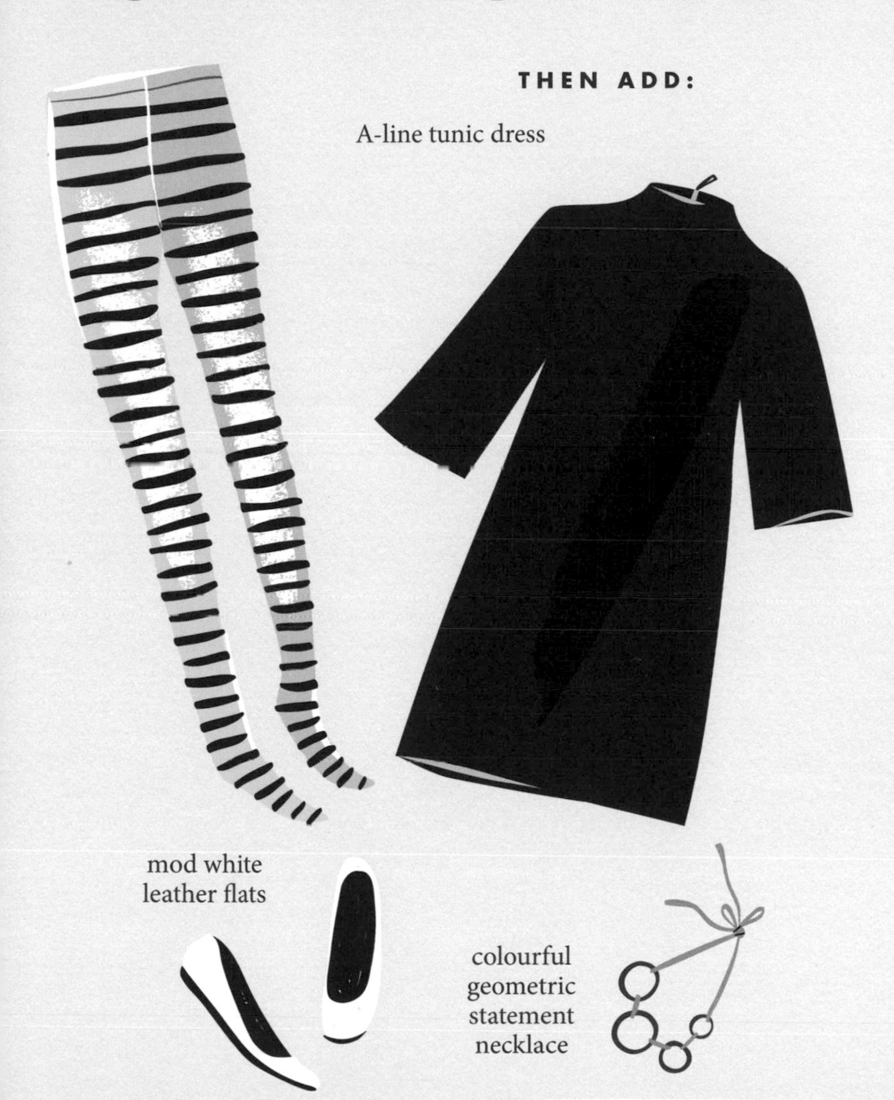

START WITH A

Striped Shorts Suit

THEN ADD:

crisp, white button-down

light leather handbag

light leather heeled slides

oversized sunglasses

simple, gold necklace

Style Icon

ALEXA CHUNG

Alexa Chung is one of the United Kingdom's finest fashion exports. The London model is known for her TV presenting gigs, fashion collabs, celebrated style book, shopping app, and fledgling (and thoroughly English) brand. She is also a master stripes wearer.

Chung began modelling at 16 but, after four successful years, she leveraged her notoriety into a media career, becoming an influencer in the truest sense of the word. With 2.3 million followers on Instagram, and a number of covers and main features in Vogue (either as a writer, or starring herself), if Chung wears it, you can bet it'll sell out in minutes. No wonder she has since scooped luxury brand campaigns, a Mulberry bag named in her honour, and the annual British Style Award from 2010 to 2013.

The everlasting buzz around street style has no doubt contributed to Chung's popularity, she is one of the most photographed style stars, as popular in the US as she is the UK. Although Chung's style has matured in recent years, becoming a little more slick and luxury, a sense of humour always brings a freshness to her look – and her label. Cheeky slogan tees, striped shirt dresses, vintage denim, mud-splattered PVC pants at Glastonbury; chic pieces are clashed with surprise additions, a pink lingerie dress with hi-top Converse, or a Breton top with black leather short shorts. Chung once described her personal look as 'ripping off Jane Birkin', and it's true there's a retro French-English vibe going on, but Chung has star power of her own: consider the trends she helped kick-start: women's brogues, pinafores, Peter Pan collars, smock dresses, and – of course – nautical stripes.

START WITH A

Striped Cropped Sleeveless Blouse

THEN ADD:

START WITH A

Striped Linen Pocket Dress

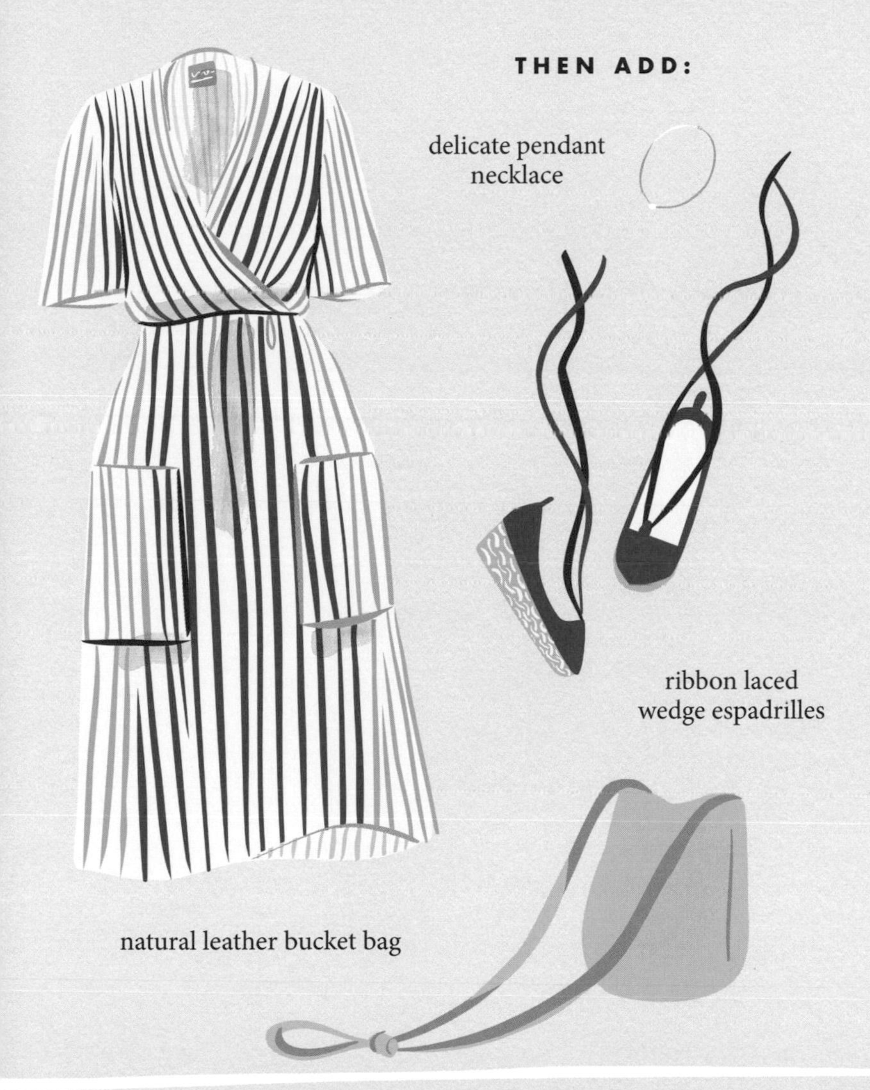

START WITH A

Striped Jersey Blazer

THEN ADD:

chambray shirt

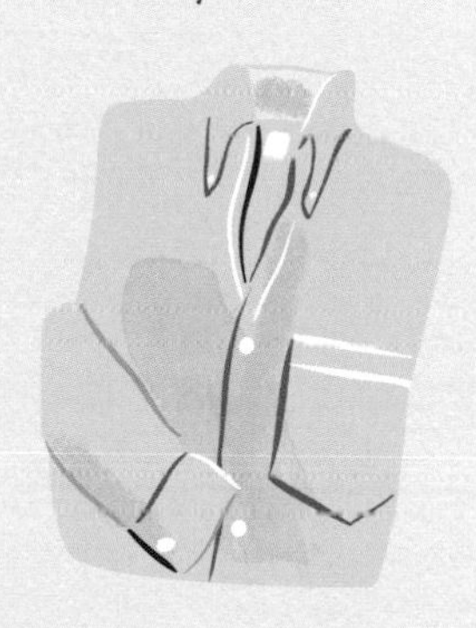

dark-rinse skinny jeans

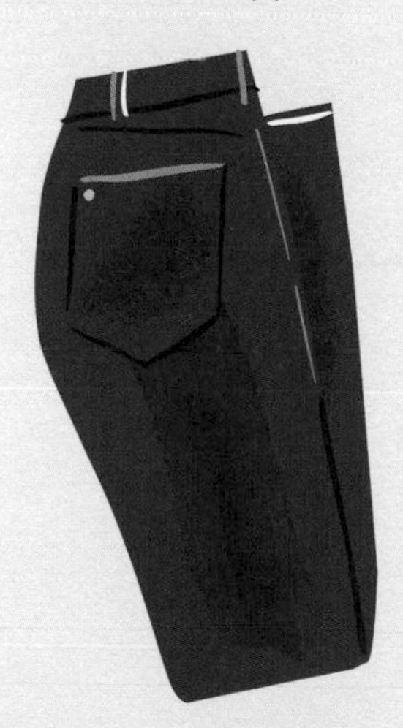

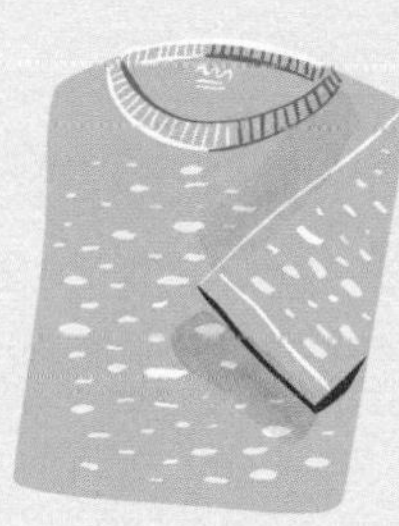

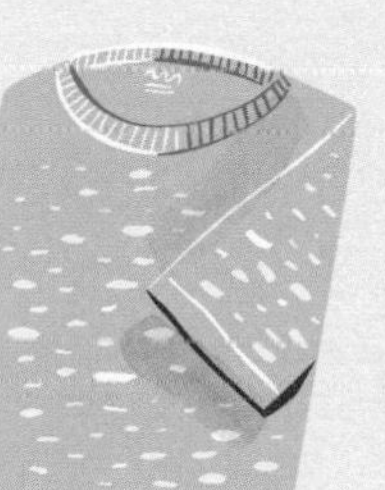

heather grey T-shirt

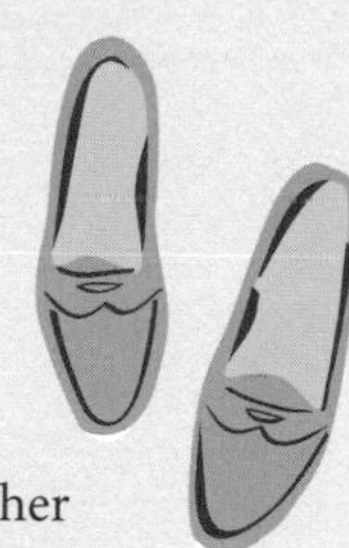

light leather loafers

Style Icon

SARAH JESSICA PARKER

The enduring influence of HBO's seminal late-90s girl power mega hit, *Sex and the City*, can be measured in its never-ending trail of memes, sassy gifs, and ironic Samantha-quote Etsy merch. Although the show itself might feel a little dated, the style of its leading lady: Sarah Jessica Parker and her alter-ego Carrie Bradshaw, feels as fresh as ever. Seriously. You will never tire of SJP's IRL outfits, or flicking through Carrie's back catalogue of loopy costume changes via Instagram account @everyoutfitonsatc (it has hundreds of thousands of followers). On screen and off, Sarah Jessica Parker has mastered the power of the stripe, and she knows how to make her shirts, skirts, and Breton tops work harder than anyone else.

It was stylist and costumier Patricia Field who created the SATC look, using its characters as a style mood board, with Carrie as her wild card. Field dressed her in all manner of maddeningly brilliant concoctions, from Westwood corsets to a Comme des Garçons afghan: luxury brands mashed up with board shorts, snake skin boob tubes, novelty handbags, angora baker boy caps, and Bavarian national dress (because, why not?).

Post-SATC, Sarah Jessica Parker has springboarded off into her own style realm, powered by Breton stripes, faded denim, cute threadbare sweats, and interdimensional couture gowns for red carpet events. In recent years, fragrances, fashion collabs, and her own footwear line have launched in between award-winning acting work, producing, and fleeting front row appearances where her (always amazing, often striped) outfits are dissected with feverish obsession.

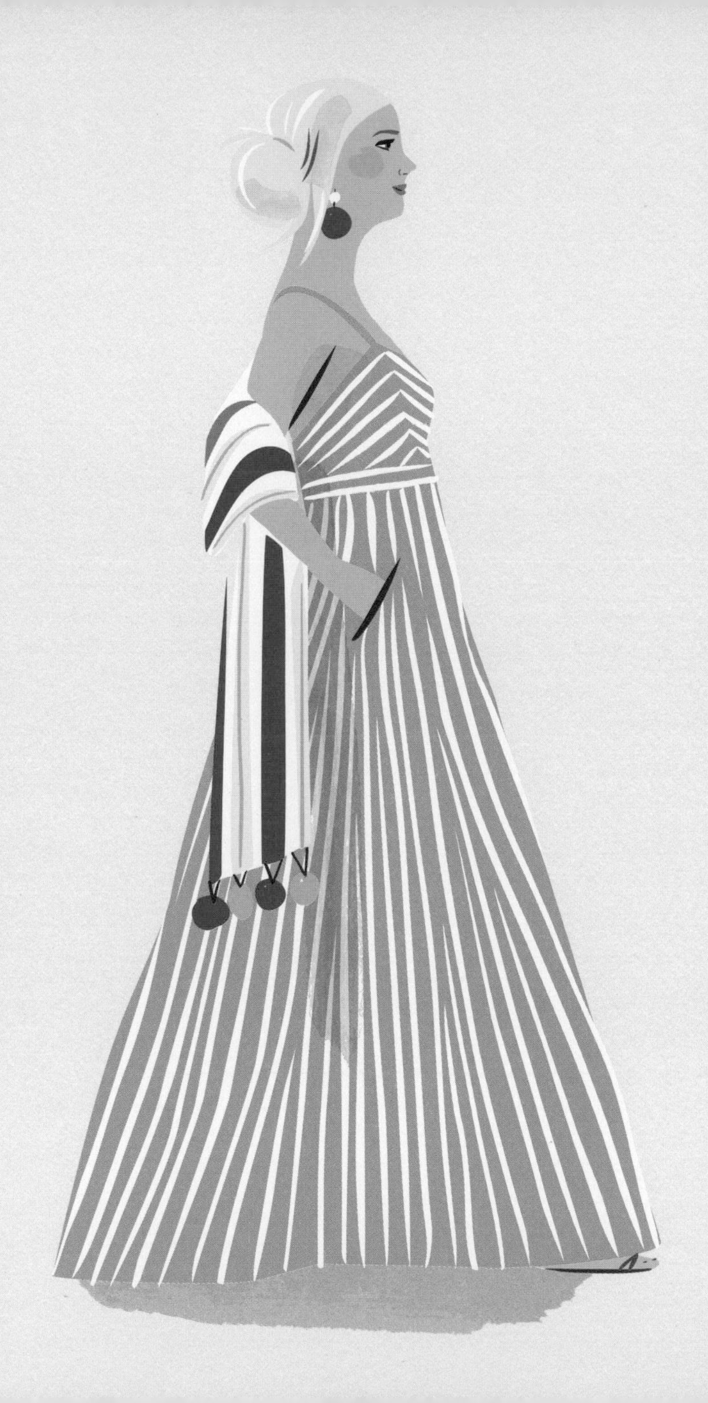

START WITH A

Summery Striped Cotton Maxi Dress

START WITH A

Striped Mod Shift Dress

THEN ADD:

clear acrylic wristlet

striped coin purse

colourful hoop earrings

colourful ankle booties

START WITH A

Crisp Pinstripe Wrap Blouse

THEN ADD:

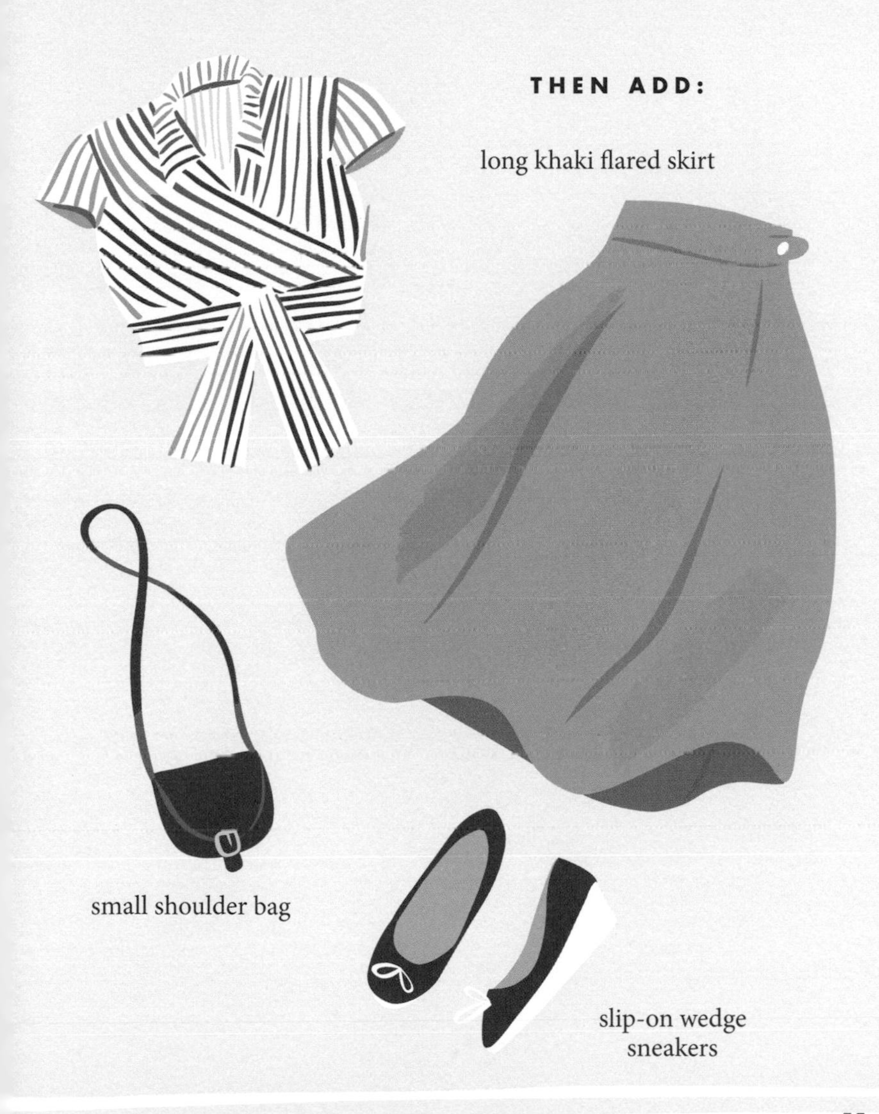

Style Icon

JANE BIRKIN

Jane Birkin is a woman who is truly comfortable with herself. The softly tousled hair, the sleepy eyes, the oversized men's clothes: her spirit animal is, hands down, a chaise longue, in slightly faded velvet. For more than half a century, the actor, singer, philanthropist and charity worker, and original It Girl, has emanated an accidentally sexy vibe that many try to copy, but few can master. It's something about the eyelash-grazing bangs and the gravity-defying cheekbones. Oh, and the deft use of stripes.

Born in 1946, Birkin was at the epicentre of 1960s Swinging London, popping up at the best parties and happenings, in cult films, and finally in the arms of Serge Gainsbourg. Her style was all about comfort and a little Annie Hall-style gender bending. Men's trousers, chunky knits, flowing shirts, ribbed tees, and pale trench coats, belted at the waist. Stripes were a go-to, a reference to Breton style as Birkin transformed into a Frenchified woman. She has been something of a style icon ever since, inspiring stylists and designers who try to touch upon Birkin's laidback look. In early 80s, Hermès created the Birkin bag, the world's most lusted-after accessory.

Birkin's personal style continues to excite and inspire. While most Birkin bag owners care for theirs obsessively (they cost upwards of $30K), Birkin's own original version is delightfully studded with beads and stickers. In these little ways, Birkin turns away from fleeting trends and gaudy glamour, maintaining a sort of anti-fashion style that's been her own for decades: stripes and shirts, baggy trousers, old scuffed Converse, and a lifetime of effortless cool.

START WITH AN

Overlapped Pinstripe Blouse

THEN ADD:

START WITH A

Striped Sweater Dress

THEN ADD:

khaki trench coat

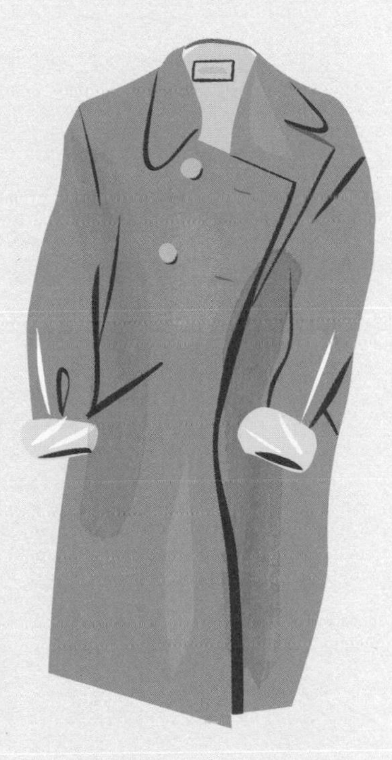

black leggings

suede lace up boots

mini cross-body leather purse

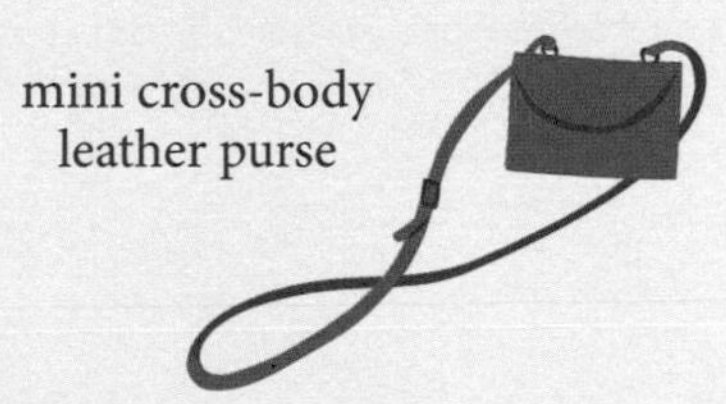

START WITH A

Boldly Striped Cocktail Dress

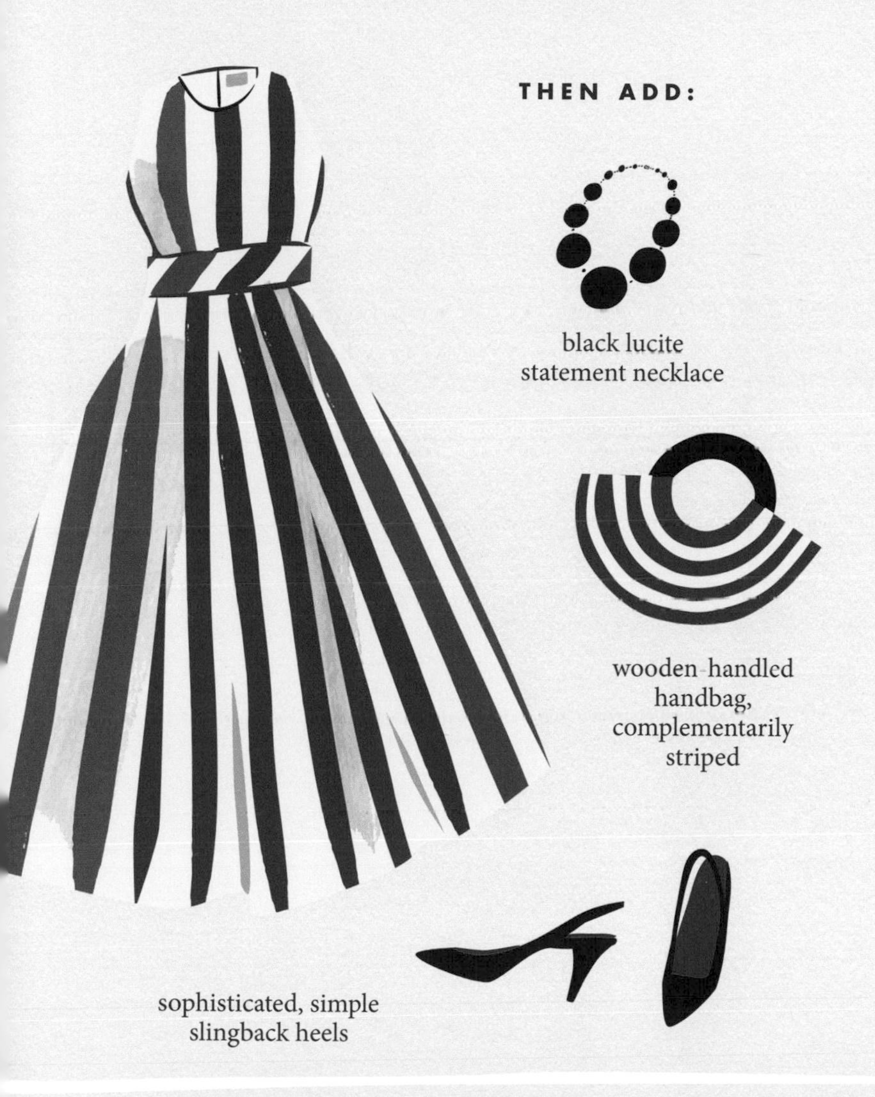

Style Icon

COCO CHANEL

The woman who started it all. Gabrielle 'Coco' Chanel, born in 1883 to the humblest of beginnings, founded fashion's most enduring and influential brand, offering a blueprint to true style that many (if not all of us) follow to some degree. Helping create the industries of ready-to-wear clothing, fragrance, jewellery, and accessories, Coco's influence and ambition saw a life writ large; she was an unstoppable creative force, picking up professional rivalries and controversy along the way. She also helped mark out the Breton top style shorthand for easy, breezy, chic.

Drawing inspiration from the British elitist fascination towards horses, yachting, and shooting, Chanel's love of sporting pursuits informed her designs. The Breton top, the most essential French item, was part of Coco's nautical look, and the stripe quickly gained its fashion credentials. In 1925, Coco launched her now legendary suit with collarless jacket and fitted skirt. It was an audacious design, borrowing from menswear, and offered a practical and comfortable alternative to the corseted, sculpted silhouette of Twenties womenswear. The Little Black Dress was another Coco invention: she created a simple jersey dress one chilly day; the compliments she received encouraged her to include the design in her collections.

Although her trademark Chanel suits, the little black dress, and quilted handbags are considered Coco's most important legacy, but the Breton top is a subtler, often overlooked Chanel essential.

START WITH A

Striped Belted Shirtdress

THEN ADD:

soft black leather satchel

black lace-up pumps

START WITH

Striped High-Waisted Swim Bottoms

THEN ADD:

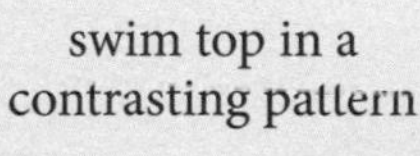
swim top in a contrasting pattern

wide-brimmed sun hat

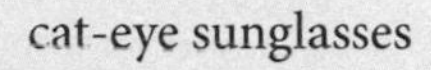
cat-eye sunglasses

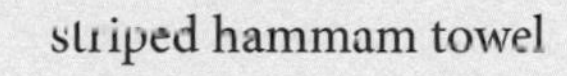
striped hammam towel

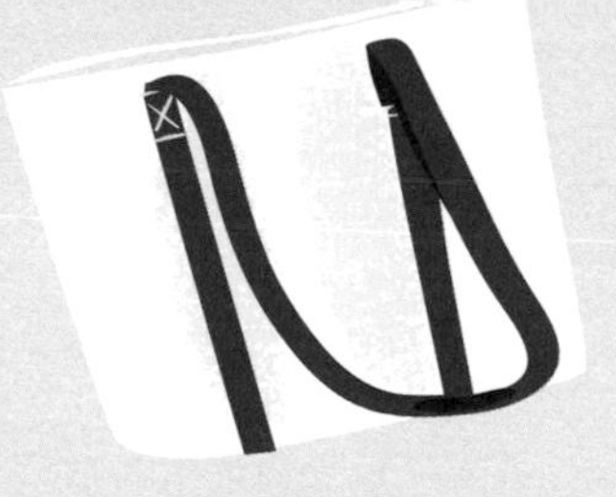

large cotton tote

START WITH A

Striped Cotton Boatneck Top

Style Icon

SOFIA COPPOLA

The ultimate poster girl for grown-up indie girls, filmmaker Sophia Coppola is the creator of heart-stopping, era-defining films, from *The Virgin Suicides* to *Lost in Translation*. Like Wes Anderson, Coppola's own left-field style is synonymous with her cinematic work; she dresses like a character in a Sofia Coppola film, and is just as shy and mysterious as her leading ladies.

Coppola's wears a de facto uniform of unpretentious, crisp separates, with tasteful polka dots, a lot of navy and, of course, stripes. A Charvet men's shirt is a Coppola essential, as are Acne jeans, cashmere socks, and the odd Alexander Wang T-shirt dress – nothing too showy. It's no wonder Coppola has an eye for style. Born into the Coppola filmmaking family, she was surrounded by stylish folk from a young age, interning at Chanel as a teenager, reading Brit fashion mag The Face, once sitting on Andy Warhol's knee.

Coppola's chic approach earned her a place in *Vanity Fair*'s Fashion Hall of Fame in 2007, a year after her first collaboration with Louis Vuitton, just after the release of *Marie Antoinette*. Through her friend Marc Jacobs (then the brand's Creative Director) Coppola co-created a bag – and she was invited back to do it again in 2016.

Coppola loves to sport a stripe, a Breton stripe to be exact. A white and navy Breton t-shirt dress or slouchy top is always acccessorised simply (albeit with a rather expensive Louis Vuitton bag); she switches to a navy and red version or a bright bumblebee black and yellow. For Coppola, as a writer and director, the simple stripe communicates a certain practicality; on her it becomes the ultimate artist's workwear.

bonjou

START WITH A

Striped Ruffled Off-the-Shoulder Top

THEN ADD:

START WITH A

Striped Vintage Playsuit

THEN ADD:

long striped scarf to wear as a head wrap

slip-on cotton sneakers

START WITH A

Skinny Striped Turtleneck

Style Icon

LINDA RODIN

Linda Rodin is the cult NYC stylist and beauty superhero whose ageless, carefree style flips a manicured finger to our expectations of how mature women should look. Her approach is refreshingly capricious: mixing modern pieces with wonderfully worn flea-market finds, vintage fabrics, and the undeniably chic power of the Breton stripe.

Rodin's brand (launched from her kitchen in 2007) is powered by a specially-formulated beauty oil, a version of which Rodin has been making for years. Otherwise, a wardrobe cultivated with beautiful and bold pieces, haggled out of the hands of New York's toughest vintage dealers, worn with fresh, contemporary clothing, is precisely where Rodin's at.

Rodin was an artist's model and photographer before her sister informed her that her photos, like her cooking, were terrible. But her styling? Exceptional. As a freelance stylist, Rodin has worked for American Harper's Bazaar, Italian Vogue, and has styled celebs from Madonna to Bob Dylan.

Today, Rodin is having a bit of a moment: her brand has become a luxury essential, and her Instagram followers are off the charts. She's a modern taste-maker, and years of developing her own personal style (rather than following fashion too closely), have seen her develop 'an eye' for what looks 100 per cent amazing. She wears the softest, most gorgeously faded pre-loved denim (she loves Levi's 501s) with the fresh power-punch of Breton stripes, and dresses up the look with her statement tinted eyewear, hot pink lips, and a clever accessory, from a vintage neck piece or tangle of thrift store pendants, to her beloved poodle, Winks.

START WITH

Skinny-Striped Trouser Socks

THEN ADD:

START WITH A

Striped Accordian-Pleated Midi Skirt

THEN ADD:

earrings with a subtle stripe motif

fitted black mock turtleneck

colourful handbag

strappy gladiator heels

START WITH A

Bold Blue Striped Boatneck Top

THEN ADD:

monochrome cotton
neckerchief

cuffed buttonfly
white denim

Ibiza-inspired boho sandals

Style Icon

MADONNA

History has blessed us with many, many Madonnas. From the trashy virgin bride at the first ever MTV Video Music Awards in 1984 (where Madonna wore a white lace lingerie wedding dress), to the Jean-Paul Gaultier conical boobed superhero of 1990, to the leotard-wearing personal trainer with cheesy dancer's fishnets in 2005, right through to butt-cheek flasher at the 2016 Met Gala. But let's head back to the early years where Madonna, then a naughty NYC guttersnipe on the brink of fame, rocked a rough-edged, girl-gone-bad look, powered by stripes. In the iconic video for 'Papa Don't Preach' (1986), she coined an iconic, boyish look: high waist stone wash denim jeans, cropped bleached hair, a battered leather Perfecto jacket slung over one shoulder, and a slouchy, open neck Breton top, (topped off with a pair of Hagrid-style bushy brows).

Strutting around the streets of Brooklyn as the quintessential teen in trouble, Madonna played on the striped top's punk credentials. As a chic, nautical item steeped in Gallic history, she helped underline its other side: a tough ass, anti-establishment essential worn by everyone from James Dean to the Ramones. Or was it Herb Ritts who created Madonna's most iconic Breton-themed image? Ritts loved working with Madonna; he masterminded her *True Blue* (1986) album cover, directed the video for 'Cherish' (1989), and shot her memorably in a traditional striped top and sailor pants, a beret and smouldering cigarette.

Haven't seen 'Papa Don't Preach' in a while? Treat yourself. Madonna looks powerful, vulnerable, and jaw-droppingly beautiful. And if there's a better way to wear stripes, we'd like to see it.

START WITH A

Peter Pan Collared Striped Sweater

START WITH A

Blue Pinstripe Button-Down

THEN ADD:

chunky plastic glasses

pencil skirt
with a bold
floral print

sleek, boxy leather clutch

white heels with
girly details

STRIPE BRANDS

Armor-Lux

Brittany-based undies-maker Armor-Lux has catered to the most Gallic of gussets since 1938, launched its first ready-to-wear collection of marinières and sweaters in the 70s – and has never looked back. Beloved in France (Armor-Lux makes SNCF's train controllers uniforms), the brand's Breton tops for men and women are traditionally-made and 100% authentic. Find them in at indie boutiques around the world, or at **@armorluxofficiel**

Madewell

J Crew's cooler little sister, Madewell, is a maker of all things denim, and the iconic pieces to wear with them. Little wonder, then, that the brand returns to the marinière season after season. Using traditional workwear and military outfitting as a starting point, but approaching it in fresh and rather contemporary ways, Madewell is the modern Breton's perfect fit. **@madewell**

Maison Labiche

Best-buddies Jenny Richard, a designer, and Marie Welté, a stylist, founded Maison Labiche in Paris after developing a signature tee with their own quirky embroidery techniques. Using song lyrics, sayings and sassy slogans – and a growing roster of designer collaborations – Maison Labiche tees are classic marinieres with a twist. **@maisonlabiche**

A.P.C.

Since 1987, Jean Touitou's impossibly cool French brand is known for its simplistic, pared-down, and modern aesthetic. Look out for A.P.C.'s cultish denim jeans, checked shirts, cute tees and tops – with the marinière popping up most seasons. The A.P.C. silhouette is always slim and contemporary, but its collections feel both nostalgic and timeless. **@apc_paris**

Saint James

Since 1889, Saint James has woven some of the world's finest knits from its Normandy-based factory, and has become synonymous with the Breton shirt. Originally using wool from the salty sheep that would graze near the shores of the village of Saint-James, the brand's first spinning mill opened in 1889, and the marinière became one of their most popular exports. Little has changed, although the Breton top is now created in a delightfully thick cotton jersey. **@saintjames**

Margaret Howell

This delightful British brand has preoccupation with vintage workwear. Designing for men and women, Margaret Howell has a craftsperson's approach and was drawn into fashion by the practicality and structure of men's clothes – and soon found that women wanted them too. Naturally, the Breton top, perfectly rendered, is a reoccurring item in Howell's collections.
@margarethowellltd

Petit Bateau

Something's wrong when your baby looks cooler than you do. Blame Petit Bateau, the more-than-120-year-old French clothing and underwear brand, that's become the last word in chic. Known for its childrenswear, in the mid-90s Karl Lagerfeld dressed Claudia Schiffer in a PB tee under a Chanel suit, and suddenly the brand was on the map.
@petitbateau

Orcival

Since 1939, French manufacturer Orcival has created not only the marinière, but its own cotton fabrics. Using vintage looms – some from the late 1800s – Orcival's USP is its hardwearing, homespun fabrics,

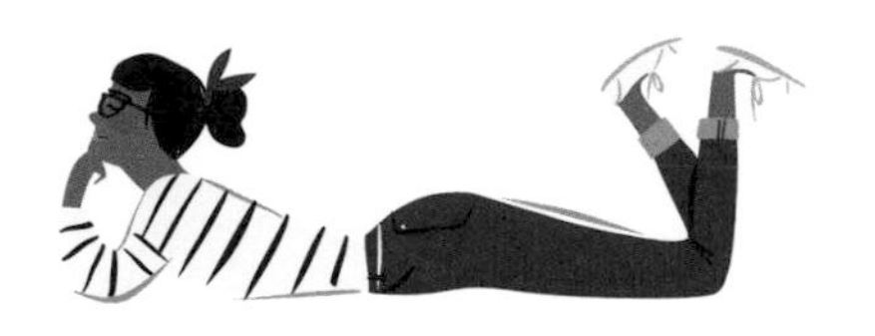

the most famous of which is known (mysteriously) as Rachel. Orcival tops keep their shape and pattern, no matter how hard you push them. Stripes to stretch it out in.
@orcival_france

Mon Breton

Hopelessly romantic/attention-seeking? Super chic marinière brand Mon Breton will monogram your Breton top, ethically-sourced in Brittany, with whoever's name you like. Amongst Mon Breton's designs of animals and flowers, get your crush's name emblazoned across your chest (caution: there's a fine line between cute and creepy).
@monbreton

Être Cécile

In a city not usually known for its humour, Paris-inspired brand Être Cécile, has a playful, confident approach to design. Lucky, then, that it was founded in London by creatives whose French approach have seen them create a lauded top, tee and clothing collection with slogans, stripes, and bright, whimsical prints that are just the right side of chic. **@etre_cecile**

THE ART OF STRIPES

First published in 2018 by Hardie Grant Books, an imprint of Hardie Grant Publishing

Hardie Grant Books (UK)
52-54 Southwark Street
London SE1 1UN

Hardie Grant Books (Australia)
Ground Floor, Building 1
658 Church Street
Melbourne, VIC 3121

hardiegrantbooks.com

British Library Cataloguing-in-Publication Data. A catalogue record for this book is available from the British Library.

ISBN: 978-1-78488-151-1

Publisher: Kate Pollard
Commissioning Editor: Kajal Mistry
Desk Editor: Molly Ahuja
Publishing Assistant: Eila Purvis
Illustrator: Libby VanderPloeg
Art Direction: Libby VanderPloeg
Colour Reproduction by p2d

Printed and bound at Leo Paper Group